THE MISSING SNOWMAN

Story by Maria Tropea

Illustrated by A. Tallarico

Derrydale Books

COPYRIGHT © 1991 KIDSBOOKS, INC.
THIS 1991 EDITION PUBLISHED BY DERRYDALE BOOKS
DISTRIBUTED BY OUTLET BOOK COMPANY, INC.
A RANDOM HOUSE COMPANY, 225 PARK AVENUE SOUTH
NEW YORK, NY 10003

PRINTED AND BOUND IN THE U.S.A.

ISBN 0-517-06142-2

ANSWERS ON THE LAST PAGE

One snowy morning, Max and his best friend Mikey built a great big snowman.

"Let's call him...Sam," said Max, as he tied Mikey's scarf around the snowman's neck.

"O.K." said Mikey. "Sam, we'll see you tomorrow."

LOOK AND LOOK AGAIN for at least 15 things that are wrong with this picture.

The next day, Sam was gone!

"Sam's disappeared!" shouted Max. "We've got to find him."

"Let's run over to Sally's Hill," said Mikey. "Maybe one of our friends has seen him."

LOOK AND LOOK AGAIN
for the following things hidden in this picture:
Fish Shovel Lost mitten Bat Flower
Bird Pail Star Paintbrush Heart Car
Football Key Flowerpot Feather

"Where else would a snowman go?" asked Mikey.

"How about ice skating?" said Max. "Snowmen must like ice."

At the ice rink, the boys saw their friend, Annie, who had carved Sam's picture in the ice with her skates.

"Does he look like this?" asked Annie. "He slid right past me a little while ago."

In addition to "Snow," LOOK AND LOOK AGAIN for at least 15 things that begin with the letter "S."

"Maybe Sam is watching the hockey game," said Max. "Let's go!" said Mikey. "The Penguins are playing the Cool Cats today."

Every penguin on the ice has an exact twin—except one. Match the twin penguins and LOOK AND LOOK AGAIN for the penguin whose twin is missing.

8

9

After watching the game, the boys were ready for something warm to drink. They kept looking for Sam as they wandered over to Charlie's Hut for some hot chocolate.

LOOK AND LOOK AGAIN for the following things in this scene:
Star Duck Top hat Leaf Quarter moon Drum
Ring Candle Fish Skis Bow tie Arrow

The boys left Charlie's feeling much warmer. Suddenly, they saw a snowman's footprints.
"Hey!" cried Max. "Sam was here! He went...that way!"

As you follow the trail, LOOK AND LOOK AGAIN for lots of things along the way.

GO!

STOP and FIND **3** BATS

GO!

GO!

GO!

STOP and FIND **6** FISH

GO!

HURRY!

GO!

STOP and FIND **2** TOP HATS

GO!

HURRY!

HURR

13

Mikey and Max followed the footprints to the top of a hill filled with skiers.

"The quickest way to get to the bottom is to ski there," said Mikey. "So, let's go!"

"Right! replied Max. "Sam's probably down there already."

LOOK AND LOOK AGAIN
for the following things on the ski slope:

Candle   Lost boot   Pillow   Mouse
Roller skates   Surfboard   Feather   Socks
Cactus   Carrot   Fire hydrant   TV set
Boom box   Banana peel   Seal   Necktie
Count Dracula   Lost mitten   Red balloon

15

At the bottom of the slope, Max and Mikey skied over to an ice-cream wagon.

"How can you sell ice cream on a cold day like this?" asked the boys.

"I'm Nutty Ned," answered the ice-cream man, "and I'll tell you something even nuttier. I just met a snowman who doesn't like the cold."

LOOK AND LOOK AGAIN for at least <u>ten</u> things that don't belong in this picture.

"I can't believe it!" said Mikey as they walked through the park. "What kind of snowman doesn't like the cold?"

"Who knows?" said Max. "Hey, there's a whole bunch of snowmen. Let's check it out!"

LOOK AND LOOK AGAIN
for the two snowmen that are identical.

There was still no sign of Sam. On the way out, the boys passed the park zoo. The bears were having a party.

"That looks like Sam!" said Max.

"Not really," replied Mikey. "It's only a polar bear wearing a party hat."

LOOK AND LOOK AGAIN for the following things hidden in this picture:

Clown face   Stars (2)   Turtle   Pear   Top hat
Fish (2)   Butterfly   Flower   Bat   Kite   House
Quarter moon   Broom   Fork   Tepee   Bone   Clothespin

21

The boys sadly decided to head for home. In Max's backyard stood their clubhouse.

"Sam!" shouted Mikey and Max. "Where were you?"

"Well, I really don't like the cold," replied Sam, "so I went looking for a warmer spot. It's a bit chilly in here, but nice and cozy. In fact, it's a perfect place to spend the winter."

LOOK AND LOOK AGAIN for at least <u>17</u> things that are wrong with this picture.

p. 2-3

p. 4-5

p. 6-7

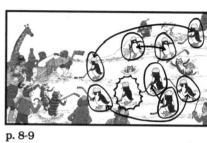

p. 8-9

p. 10-11

p. 12-13

p. 14-15

p. 16-17

p. 18-19

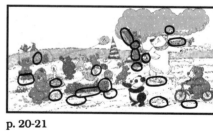

p. 20-21

p. 22-23